Love Is a Happy Cat

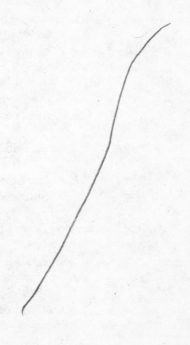

By MICHAEL W. FOX

Canine Behavior
Canine Pediatrics
Integrative Development of Brain and Behavior in the Dog
Behavior of Wolves, Dogs, and Related Canids
Understanding Your Dog
Understanding Your Cat
Concepts in Ethology: Animal and Human Behavior
Between Animal and Man: The Key to the Kingdom
The Dog: Its Domestication and Behavior
Understanding Your Pet
Returning to Eden: Animal Rights and Human Responsibility
One Earth, One Mind
The Soul of the Wolf: Observations and Meditations
How to Be Your Pet's Best Friend
Agricide—The Hidden Crisis That Affects Us All
Laboratory Animal Husbandry
The Whistling Hunters
Superdog: Raising the Perfect Canine Companion
Silent World: Genetic Engineering—Nature's End?
The New Animal Doctor's Answer Book
The Healing Touch
Love Is a Happy Cat

CHILDREN'S BOOKS
The Wolf
Vixie: The Story of a Little Fox
Sundance Coyote
Ramu and Chennai
What Is Your Dog Saying? (with Wende Devlin Gates)
Wild Dogs Three
Whitepaws: A Coyote-Dog
Lessons from Nature: Fox's Fables
The Touchlings
The Way of the Dolphin

Love Is a Happy Cat

Dr. Michael W. Fox
D.Sc., Ph.D., B.Vet.Med., M.R.C.V.S.

Cartoons by
Harry Gans

Newmarket Press
New York

This book published simultaneously in the United States of
America and in Canada.

90 91 92 93 2 3 4 5 6 7 8 9 0

Book design by Tim Gaydos

Library of Congress Cataloging in Publication Data

Fox, Michael W., 1937–
  Love is a happy cat.

  1. Cats—Quotations, maxims, etc. I. Gans,
Harry. II. Title.
PN6278.C36F69 1982 818'.5402 82-14216
ISBN 1-55704-084-2

Quantity Purchases
Companies, professional groups, clubs, and other organizations may
qualify for special terms when ordering quantities of this title. For
information, write to Special Sales Department, Newmarket Press,
18 East 48th Street, New York, N.Y. 10017, or call (212) 832-3575.

Manufactured in the United States of America

For all cats, wild and tame

ACKNOWLEDGMENTS

The author wishes to express his gratitude to his wife, Deborah, whose original idea it was to do this book. He also wishes to thank Sylvie Reice, his editor, for her invaluable assistance and advice, and Esther Margolis, his publisher, for her continuing support and understanding.

INTRODUCTION

I really consider myself fortunate and privileged. As a veterinarian and animal behaviorist (or more correctly, ethologist) I spend my professional life in the wonderful and often perplexing world of animals. My personal life is rich with animals too—a dog as well as two fine felines.

For me, as for many people, life would be unthinkable without cats. They enrich our lives with companionship, fun, love, and fascination. In return, we can give them love and wholesome food and veterinary care. But without a knowledge of cats' behavior, idiosyncrasies, and emotional needs, our appreciation of their "catness" will be lacking, and we will be unable to enjoy the depth, subtlety and complexity of our feline friends. We also may well fall short of being good cat caretakers without working knowledge of their wily ways and wants.

As vice president of The Humane Society of the United States, I am faced constantly with a variety of animal problems that pet owners bring to me. Most often these are "people problems." An experimental psychologist, who was doing brain research on cats, called an ethologist friend of mine to check out one of his research cats. He thought it had a respiratory problem. My friend, in shock, told the Ph.D. researcher that the cat was purring—it was expressing affection and a desire to be petted. The psychologist didn't know that cats purr!

Fortunately, not all people are as naive as this man. A couple recently called me for advice about their kitten who they thought might be mentally deranged. Every evening, the kitten would race through the house, hiding, stalking, back-arching, and clawing up the sofa—and so on. I told them that the kitten was simply playing and "hallucinating." I explained that some kittens are more active, playful, and imaginative than others, and suggested that they play with their "wild" kitten. Reassured that their cat was quite normal, they were once again a happy cat-family. Most people love their pets; they just don't comprehend how cats express needs and emotions.

I never cease to be amazed at some people's lack of understanding about cats, which can lead to indifferent and even inhumane treatment. The Humane Society of the United States helped stop the publication of a calendar with color photographs of cats being tortured. The pictures were so vivid they crossed the bounds of "black humor" into sadism. Since cats are independent and have wills of their own, it's harder for many people to love them. And because cats don't return devotion in the manner of loyal dogs, they are often considered second-class citizens. "Sick" cartoons showing dogs being tortured would not go over big. Yet the fact is that cats are capable of as varied a range of emotions, possibly, as ourselves. And cats *can* show affection *if* you give them affection.

By not responding correctly to our cats' behavior we are, in effect, creating more problems. It is possible to know what a cat is feeling and what its intentions are, and in these pages, I will reveal some important facts about cat psychology and behavior. It's also possible to have fun with cats and cat-lovers, as we have illustrated in this book, without resorting to sadistic humor or ridicule. These views are what inspired me to prepare what may seem to be, at first glance, yet another cat cartoon book. But, as you will soon see, *Love Is a Happy Cat* is meant to be more than funny.

I hope this book will make your cat's life happier, your relationship with your feline more satisfying, and help everyone to understand cats better. After all, a cat is a cat is a cat! That's what cat-loving is all about.

M.W.F.

Love is
respecting
the intrinsic
worth of cats—
not as status symbols,
conversation pieces,
or toys
for children.

Love is never
   having to be friendly
      to strangers
         whom I happen
            to dislike
               or fear.

Love is neutering
a tomcat so
he doesn't have to
go out and get
beaten up each night
to prove
his macho.

Love is
a scratch-post
to claw on
when I'm excited,
showing off,
or sharpening
my toenails
(especially
if I'm confined
indoors!).

Love is
a high place
  to climb on
and look
    down at
      the world.

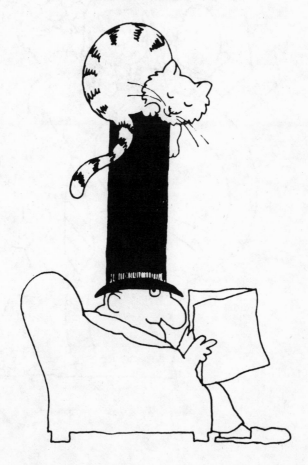

Love means
   giving a kitten contact
      with a variety of people,
      children included,
         so that later in life
      it won't fear strangers
or become a recluse.

Love is
not being petted
when
I'm in the mood
to be left alone
to meditate
or think about
nothing.

Love is not letting me
manipulate you
into feeding me
only tuna or chicken
instead of
a complete and
balanced diet.

Love is
rejecting
the foolish myths
that we practice
black magic
and do harm
to newborn babies.
A cat is not a vampire—
a cat is a
companion.

Love is
having
regular shots and
check-ups,
even if I hiss
at the doctor
or try
to hide.

Love is realizing
        that a cat is a cat—
a creature with
            idiosyncrasies
                to be enjoyed
        and understood,
                not controlled
                    or dominated.

Love is appreciating
the paradoxical
nature of cats:
we love whom
we choose, and we
are dependent
upon no one.

Love is
a bag
of catnip
to get
high on.

Love is
a walk
outdoors
to check up
on the world...
but for
heaven's sake,
don't forget
my harness
and leash.

Love is
looking out
for your
cat's tail
when you
shut doors—
especially
refrigerator
doors.

Love is
neutering
your cat
so she won't
come into heat and
roll and yowl in frustration;
love is not adding a litter
to the millions of
unwanted kittens
that are born
every
year.

Love is
a ready supply
of fresh
grass or sprouted
wheat to nibble.
(Did you know
it's good
for my health?)

Love is
knowing that
when I flop
over onto
one side
at your feet
I'm saying,
"Play with me."

Love is
never
having
to wear
a flea collar
because
they make
cats sick.

Love is
not punishing
me if I stop
using the
litter tray.
Maybe my bladder hurts
and I need a vet;
or maybe I'm jealous
of the TLC
you're giving the
new baby or kitten.

Love is
     not being sent
to a boarding kennel
     when you go on vacation
     but having a sitter
     to look after me.

Love is
not having
a bath
like a dog,
except when
my vet
prescribes it.

Love
is a
fish-tank
to
contemplate.

Love
is a
fireman,
arriving
in the
nick
of time.

Love is
knowing
that when
I hiss
I'm scared
or angry,
so don't take
it as rejection,
or punish me
for being
honest.

Love is
        knowing that
a harsh voice
        and a direct stare
is discipline enough—
        no need to hit me
or rub my nose
        into any mess
    I might
        accidentally
    make.

Love is
understanding
that cats
aren't
distant and aloof,
but independent
and
self-reliant.

Love-bites
are not meant
        to hurt you—
please, forgive me
    if I get
        carried away.
A little tap
        on the nose
    will restrain
            me.

Love is
respecting
the fact that
some
independent
felines just
don't take
to being
cuddled.

Love is
understanding
that,
like you,
we often get
carried
away
by our
instincts.

Love is
my owners
buying up
all copies
of sick humor
cat books
and my shredding
them into
cat
litter.

Love is trusting me
when I act wild and get
my "night-time crazies"—
I'm just having fun
and hallucinating,
and I don't need
a tranquilizer.

Love is
providing me
with feline TV
in the form of
a bird feeder
outside
the window.

49

Loving cats
is to accept us
unconditionally, but not
to overindulge us . . .
cupboard love
makes fat cats.

Love is
one of your
old socks to
carry around
like a substitute
kitten
or even
a mouse.

Love is
not breeding
for
"sophistication
and
refinement,"
but for
health and normalcy.
Who needs deformed heads,
frail limbs,
and
genetic defects?

Love is
    having a companion
        kitten for company:
    two cats are happier
        and healthier than
            one, but...

... Love is *not* having
a companion kitten
forced on me when
I'm old and too set
in my ways
to accept a
newcomer.

Love is
understanding that
when I scrape around
my food bowl,
I'm not disturbed
with the smell but want
to cover it up so
no one will steal
the remains.

Love is
not withdrawing when
I rub against you
with the scent from
my head and lips;
that's just how I mark
my friends.

Love is
getting me spayed if I
have a false pregnancy.
(You'll know when I adopt
inanimate objects as
kitten substitutes,
and even begin
to produce milk!)

Love is
adopting
a homeless kitten
from the
humane
society.

Love
is a
cardboard
box
to hide
in.

Love
is a
clean
litter
box.

Love is
a carpeted
   shelf by the
windowsill
   so I can bask
in the sun.

Loving
cats
entails recognizing
that, like humans,
we can suffer from
emotional as well as
physical problems,
including allergies,
depression, and flu.
(We'll even
pull out our fur
when we're
extremely
upset!)

Love is giving me
some toys to
chase and kill
so that when I feel
the urge to hunt,
I won't leap and
nip at your legs
from a
hiding place.

Love is
sitting on top
of your
book
while you're
reading.

Love is
being allowed
to take your
warm spot
on the sofa
when you
get up.

Love is
knowing I'll be fed
at a regular time
and your taking care
not to step on me
as I steer you
to the
kitchen.

Love is
the smell of
fish frying
and the certainty
of a nibble
when they're
ready.

Love is
knowing
that I don't
bring bad luck
just because I
happen to be
black.

Love is
not letting
  me out
to roam
  the
neighborhood.
  (Do you
want me
  to get hit
by a car,
  chased
by dogs,
  and/or
beaten up
  by tough
territorial
  toms?)

When I look at you
  and close my eyes,
don't ever think
  I'm ignoring you
or acting aloof;
  I'm just relaxing
because I love
  being with you.

Love is
a regular
massage by
my owner
because
it's so
relaxing.

Love is
realizing that
when we twitch
and mew in our
sleep, we're just
dreaming.
Don't
you?

Love is
knowing that
cats are
impeccably clean,
and that a cat
who doesn't
groom itself
must be
sick!

Love is a trapper
      who stops trapping
wild animals for their fur,
      knowing that they suffer
and that cats get into
      their traps
         as well.

Love is
being
groomed
every day
with a
soft
brush.

Love is
not dumping
a litter of kittens
but finding
them good
homes.

Love is
a new taste treat
every once in a while—
like some tidbits
from your
dinner plate?

Love is
a responsible human
who calls the authorities
when he observes
a cat being neglected
or abused by someone
in the community.

Love is
putting me
to sleep and
out of anguish
when the vet
says it is time
and I'm
incurably
ill.

Love
is a
cat-mobile
with
fun things
to swipe,
catch,
bat, and
bite.

Love is
understanding
that cats have
the capacity
to reason;
we know
when a bark
has nothing
to do with
a bite.

Love is
letting me sit
on a
brand-new
skirt or sweater
that you have
just laid out
on the
bed.

Love is
a driver who
picks up a stray
or injured cat
from the
roadside and
takes it
to the
animal
shelter.

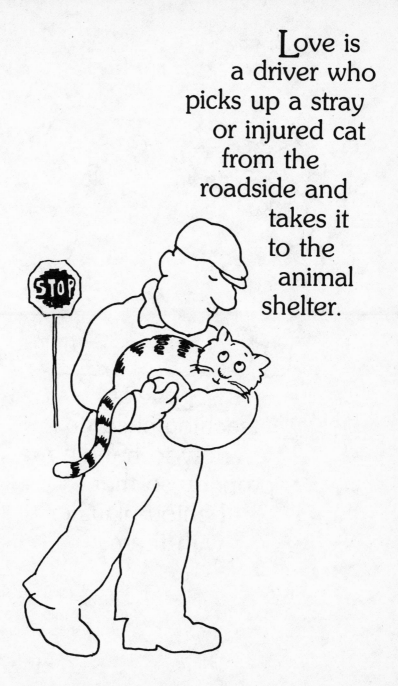

Love is
teaching children
    how to handle me
properly so that
    I enjoy playing
    with them.

Love is
letting me
sleep on
your back
or stomach
when I want
to feel
close.

Love is
knowing
that when I'm
embarrassed
and have been
reprimanded
I "groom" myself
briefly and
intensely.

Love is
knowing
puppies
will take off,
but kittens
need to
stay and nurse
with mama
for at least
eight
weeks.

Love is
knowing
that when I
stick my rump
in your face,
I'm just being
submissive
and kittenish,
not trying
to seduce
you.

Loving
is treating me
like a cat
and not like
a little
person.

Love is
your old
sweater
to lie on
when
you're
away.

No—I'm not
   perverted when I
respond to
   your embrace by
drooling and
   kneading you with
my front paws,
   I'm just acting
like a kitten
   again and
   I love it!

Love is
not putting off
a trip to
the veterinarian
when
I'm sick
(because
I can
get
sicker).

Love is
understanding
that we're not
being naughty
or klutzy when
we knock
things over,
we're just
desperate
for our
owner's
attention!

Love is
leaving us be:
we're not
all of us outgoing,
but creatures
of many
temperaments
and many
moods.

Love is
protecting
us from
needles and pins,
electric fans
and cords,
household chemicals
and other
hazards.

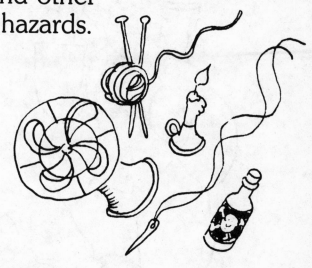

Love is
a landlord
who lets tenants
keep cats, knowing
that they neither
bring in dirt
and vermin,
nor destroy
property.

Love is
greeting me
with a few strokes
when you
come home
because I've been
looking
forward
all day
to your
arrival.

Love is
harmonizing
with the
mind of the cat—
totally
relaxed,
yet fully
alert.

Love is
realizing that
when you tickle
my tummy or the base of
my tail it sometimes
feels so intense
I can't stand it!
Don't feel hurt
if I hiss and
swipe or
run off.

Love is
catching on
that sometimes
I like to
show off and be
the center of
attention.

LOVE FOR CATS
is part of a
universal love
for all creatures
which impels
us toward a
reverence
for all life.

About the Author

Dr. Michael W. Fox, D.Sc., Ph.D., B.Vet.Med., M.R.C.V.S., a strong animal rights advocate, is Director of the Center for Respect of Life and Environment and is a vice president of The Humane Society of the United States. The author of more than thirty books, both scientific and popular—including *The Healing Touch, The New Animal Doctor's Answer Book, Understanding Your Cat,* and *Understanding Your Dog*—Dr. Fox is also a regular contributor to *McCall's* Magazine and has a nationally syndicated newspaper column called "Animal Doctor." He is based in Washington, D.C.

About the Illustrator

Harry Gans, artist and illustrator, specializes in design for toys and crafts and for posters and campaigns relating to conservation and education issues. He created the cat character for *Love Is a Happy Cat* exclusively for this book. He is also the creator of Eli, the Adaptable Elephant. Mr. Gans lives in Berkeley, California, with a Manx named Max.

If you love animals, and have friends that do too, then you'll want every one of them to have copies of Dr. Michael Fox's wonderful pet care books.

LOVE IS A HAPPY CAT
Cartoons by Harry Gans

There has never been a cat care book quite like this one. Wonderfully and wittily illustrated, *Love Is a Happy Cat* captures everything that is truly important about cat care and behavior in a handful of words. If cats could write, here's what they would say about life and love. "Buy it. Read it. Give it. Don't miss this book."—*Cat Fancy* Magazine

THE HEALING TOUCH

Massaging your pet? It may sound unnecessary or even ridiculous, but in *The Healing Touch* Dr. Fox reveals in loving detail how the widely accepted new techniques he has helped pioneer over the past twenty years can help you have a happier, healthier pet. Every household with a pet—especially a cat or dog—needs this landmark book. "Contains one of the most important chapters (on diagnostic massage) ever written for the layman."—*The ASPCA Report*

THE NEW ANIMAL DOCTOR'S ANSWER BOOK
Illustrated by B. J. Lewis

Thoroughly revised with one-third entirely new material, this fascinating sourcebook, drawn from Dr. Fox's nationally syndicated column, answers more than 1,000 questions about the health, psychology, and well-being of cats, dogs, fish, birds, rabbits, hamsters, and other companion animals. "This sensible, compassionate approach to pet selection and care is a must for all animal lovers."—*ALA Booklist*

Ask for these titles at your local bookstore or use this coupon to order from Newmarket Press, 18 East 48th Street, NY, NY 10017.

Please send me:
_____copies of LOVE IS A HAPPY CAT @ $6.95 (trade paperback)
_____copies of THE HEALING TOUCH @ $10.95 (trade paperback)
_____copies of THE NEW ANIMAL DOCTOR'S ANSWER BOOK @ $14.95
    (trade paperback)

For postage and handling add $2.00 for the first book, plus $1.00 for each additional book. Allow 4–6 weeks for delivery. Prices and availability subject to change.

I enclose check or money order payable to NEWMARKET PRESS in the amount of $_____
NAME_____
ADDRESS_____
CITY/STATE/ZIP_____

For quotes on quantity purchases, or for a copy of our catalog, please write Newmarket Press, 18 East 48th Street, NY, NY 10017, or call (212) 832-3575.   HEALBOB.90